THE BIG EMPTY

and

OTHER DREAMS

by

≈ ≈ ≈ ≈ MOKASIYA ≈ ≈ ≈ ≈

*To Paul
Deep blessings in the music and the heart of belonging —
Much Love
Mokasiya*

The Big Empty and Other Dreams
Copyright © by Mokasiya

First published by Mokasiya in 2018

Previously published poetry books by the author:

Pipe, Sensuality and the Sacred
Climbing A Mesa
The Shaman's Dream
When God First Laughed

For additional copies of this or any of his books,
to sponsor a poetry reading or a play-shop,
or to reproduce any part of this book,
send your inquiries to the author at:
mokalightpoetry@gmail.com

"I Get Desperate" first appeared in Comstock Review

"Gratitude," "How Risky," and "A Heart Day"
first appeared in mokalightpoetry.wordpress.com

I am forever grateful for the editing skills of
Lynn Gray, and all the support in my writing life.

Illustrations for this book are by the artist
Jeff Sartain, to whom I feel deep gratitude for
sharing his talent and insights.

1	My Wilderness
2	How Risky
3	Longing for a Dishrag
4	Washing the Dishes
5	Untitled
6	Achieving Enlightenment
7	Walk-in
8	Can We Surrender?
9	To Know the Feel
10	Are There Coyotes?
11	*Illustration*
12	What Can I Say?
13	Sainthood
14	Mixing Paint
15	As You Taste the Moon
16	Mother Earth Speaks
17	Grandfather's Boats
18	The First Dream
19	Less Attached
20	In a Heron's Beak
21	*Illustration*
22	Silk or Ink
23	Gets Carved Out
24	Be Silent Still
25	About to Fall
26	The Bones of It
27	To Share
28	Finish that Letter
29	The Moon
30	Planting Corn
31	Peg Leg
32	Belonging
33	*Illustration*
34	I Get Desperate
35	The Big Empty
36	The Golden Laughter
37	Giving Birth
38	Beauty

39	Share Your Best
40	The Un-shamed
41	As Love Awakes
42	The Foxes
43	*Illustration*
44	Sing to the Stones
45	Brain Fog
46	Take the Wax Away
47	Elemental Gifts
48	A Place
49	*Illustration*
50	Gratitude
51	The Big Heat
52	Sing Underwater
53	Forgiveness
54	On Her Body
55	My Silver Key
56	*Illustration*
57	Light Changes Everything
58	The Wind
59	To Be Holy
60	Shall We Share?
61	Drink Good Water
62	What is Love?
63	To Aim Skyward
64	The Mind Palace
65	At the Canyon
66	*Illustration*
67	Inclusive and Free
68	Paradox Tabernacle
69	What to Consider
70	Another Life
71	Shift and Stretch
72	Playful with the Earth
73	The Stones Speak
74	As We Behold
75	Untitled
76	Where I Go To Lie Down

Introduction

Have you asked yourself, what is emptiness?

The poetry in these pages endeavors to explore the big empty and other such dreams of this unknown voyage as we weave our human life along the dance floor of this earth and our spiritual life through the often unseen and unknowable mystery we may simply call the soul.

I share these poetic musings with the intention that all beings will be moved by a practice of kindness and grace, love and joy, from the beauty way of heart and soul.

May your life be filled with joy completely, everyday in every-way, no matter how large or how small, to live in gratitude, no matter how easy or difficult the endeavor may seem.

Mokasiya

THE BIG EMPTY

and

OTHER DREAMS

by

≈ ≈ ≈ ≈ MOKASIYA ≈ ≈ ≈ ≈

This book is dedicated to heart and soul, to living a healthy life in unconditional love, and deep respect for this living, soulful Earth.

My Wilderness

I love to rise when the sun is still young
walk through the park in this desert city,
like it's a part of my *Inner Wilderness*
as I stoop to examine the owl pellets
that lie upon the ground

I stop and watch the ants move along
like thin raisins with legs,
as ground squirrels
nose out of the earth
from their underworld of possibility,
I listen to the talk of trees
eucalyptus and sycamore
and give thanks to our shared belonging,
as if the trees can understand my intention
and I can open up enough to listen
to the roots of their resolve

I touch the names and hearts
carved into their skin,
the rusted staples like tiny hopes
that held up a paper moon
or a flyer that said, *lost dog*,
I begin to remove those metallic thorns
like sandburs and scabs of my childhood,
before I walk home and bake cornbread
with green chilies and sesame seeds
to nurture my own body
in a way that says,
I love you, I am worthy
and grateful for this day.

"And the day came when the risk to remain tight in a bud was more painful than the risk it took to blossom."
— Anais Nin

How risky can life be
to gaze along the edge
of the unknowable?
like a whole universe in motion
that spins toward the unseen,
like a seed encoded
with original instructions
centered inside the soul's need

can we love ourselves without loving a god?
can we love a god without loving ourselves?
and what is love and what is god?
all the air that we breathe?
to let go of separation,
us and them, you and me?
heart and soul, great mystery?

when we open up
like a spark of light
can we shed our pain
of fight or flight?

to release—
what can this be?
the authentic self
wake up to see,
and share our life
in this vast ocean dream,
like a bud, a flower,
a free-flowing stream.

Longing for a Dishrag

Close to a prickly pear cactus,
one story tall,
are white-winged doves that circle about
like military planes in search of
a safe landing,
we sit across from one another
in the warm kitchen of silence
lost in the arc of our own thoughts,
where everything, eventually, gets spoken

It's a sunday morning to relax and speculate,
if we go to a different church every week
will we gather a broader insight
into religion or spirituality?
will our egos cling stronger
to our own hot salsa of redemption
and egg-scrambled beliefs?

This kitchen has no dishrag
like the one he learned
to braille the plates and bowls on
under the suds of his childhood,
as he longed to dash out the screen door
for a game of tag or baseball

I wonder, is there a dishrag hall of fame?
can all this kitchen talk,
our history, be washed down the drain?

Washing the Dishes

I woke up this morning and began
by shaving my body with coffee,
the warm steam of its aroma, like my hair,
curled down around the soccer game of my feet.

The toilet was gurgling out a Mozart concerto,
as the cat was playing backgammon
with a mouse.
This was all before the eggs
dove into the cast-iron skillet,
cooked themselves into an omelet of desire.

I began to feel less conceited without
my body hair,
sensing all the past dreams and possibilities
that once bathed around me, orbiting the one
secular belief of becoming more human.

I swept up the hair with a pen knife,
sliced a small hole under an apple tree
and placed the protein offering into the ground.
Nothing spectacular occurred, like Guadalupe
or Jesus or some other sacred icon
appearing on the spread of my toast.

Something small happened when the ego
sat across from my breakfast plate, offering
an olive branch in the sharp-like talon
of its beak.
We shared a wink.
It was the start of the ego
washing the dishes, leftover, in the sink.

Untitled

The koan was written backwards
on a parchment
that did not exist
as the mockingbird
sang at sunrise.

Achieving Enlightenment

I reached the highest level of enlightenment
after six decades of struggle
and numerous practices of self awareness.
There are different levels of enlightenment,
right? it's all good, right?

I became so skilled at training my mind
that I could pray the *mala* beads
in my right hand, cook lunch with my left,
while chanting *the holy name*

This got me to the fifth stage of illumination.
I entered the next phase through the teachings
of the one-step program to bliss,
but then I was stuck for a looooong time

On a whim, without any goal in mind,
I went to a tuba *kirtan* and there it happened—
full emergence into the great void of the tuba
where I received complete nirvana

I began to channel great spiritual teachers
like Lucille Ball, Red Skelton, Phyllis Diller,
and Flip Wilson—
ascended masters of the highest order,
not only filled with Christ consciousness
but also the Buddha heart

I share this revelation, or is it illusion?
as I wake up each morning
to begin from the start.

Walk-in

Do you find more possibilities
as you walk the Red Road
into the muse of your own native skin?
Danish and mixed-blood

How the drizzle moistens you,
lays along your torso
the loon cry of your voice

What's it all about
between the fool and the scapegoat
or a barbecue party of archetypes
that praises the scent of God?

You enter a cone of power
at the laundry-mat,
the spin cycle
engages the golden goblet
of your soul

You drift off to sleep
as a nightingale takes your fears away
from the crumbs on your lips

From your expression
and agreement to be a walk-in
through the portal of a dream,
your open surrender into bliss.

Can We Surrender?

So now we ride
a spiritual yak,
no holding on
or looking back

a map, a plan
as betrayal clung,
like a tangled vine
an unconscious tongue

does love cast light
upon anger's chest
the holy grail
the sacred best?

can we forgive
for forgiveness sake
accept our passion
thy beauty to make?

and as we spiral
into stardust light,
back to Source
through darkest night

on a spiritual path
to dance and play,
sing and laugh
shall we join this way?

like a core release
from the embryonic seed,
like death, like life,
can we surrender our need?

To Know the Feel

I didn't brush the ivory
of my teeth today
or sing the name
of the holy,
I felt more like smok'n whiskey
and drink'n cigarettes,
rais'n hell in the church
I seldom go to

I want the seam of you closer, Beloved,
enough to sniff
the natural flow
from your caress—
or is that too personal
like the taste of wild plums?

At home we share
what it means to split open
the first steam of hot cookies,
glutton-and gluten-free

To know the feel
of taste complete
with each moment a gift
into a kinder we.

Are There Coyotes?

In the distant dark night of sleep
I feel the sound of a train whistle
like the pliable voice of a wise elder,
like a balm that heals from the source of love

It's impossible to see the galaxy of stars
through the million blazes of artificial light
that call this desert valley home
as I long for the wilderness of bear,
mountain lion, and porcupine

In the cove of daylight
a man walks toward me
with his shaved head and muscled body
with the words JESUS SAVES tattooed along
the gleam of his shaved chest and stomach
that I find curious and unsettling

I believe there are coyotes in this city
and the man with the Jesus tattoo
may just be one of them,
as well as the shy Latina
with long white hair
and her tiny dog, whose teeth
want to bite into the thin meat of my ankles

And myself, when I refuse to stand up
for the national anthem,
having my own torch, timber, and grief
about American history, as I wonder about
this human life, a belief in faith, in all
that sweet Jesus has ever saved.

"Is it the grinding stone of shame, blame and guilt and the pure water of beauty, joy and wholeheartedness that turn the two stones to mill the golden corn of the soul?"
— Mokasiya

What can I say about vulnerability?
as I felt your hand slip into mine,
not tight or weak in its invite
but like a warm pulse, a mere entwine

A need unspoken to touch and grow
a tender embrace from the vision we sow,
to hear the heart like a song of a drum
spiral into memory, that eternal hum of
what connection means, connection becomes

Flexible at the center, same joy, same tears
at the edge of our darkest, imagined fears,
as a thin crack can open a tiny seed
lets in the light of the soul's creed

As I carry up the stones found in the river
that milled the corn, the food giver,
to place near a path, in a garden of love,
with all that's below and all that's above

To claim we are worthy,
our divinity and grace
in the dance of creation,
in heart's sacred space.

Sainthood

I've sent in my application
to become a saint,
certainly I have a great chance
of being accepted,
using a lot of "I" statements
like the self-help books speak about,
letting go of,
"you should, you could, you would
be very wise to choose me for sainthood"

I solicit this high honor
for one day
not a forever thing
or any kind of special adoration

Sainthood for a day, that's enough,
like queen or king for a day,
lay down all weapons forever day,
sacred is the whole planet day

The laughter saint—
that's it,
come on, let's play—

but only for a day?

Mixing Paint

I got my
bodhisattva certificate taken away
for my failure to read the forty-six failures
of a bodhisattva

I imagine something more positive,
playful, and tactile
besides a desire to build a practice
on a foundation of failures

I've studied the four noble turtles,
I mean truths—
and the eight foolish yaks,
I mean the eight-fold path,
as i wonder about,
the One Great Lie

The patron saint of humor is Philip Neri,
in Hindi, Lord Krishna and Ganesh
share the comedy spotlight,
and that makes sense, right?
Ganesh, a human body
with an elephant head

Today I read the heart sutra,
which speaks about emptiness,
beyond thoughts of the mind,
like letting go of a secret desire
to become a living saint,
time to go and carry water
wash up on some poetry
and mix a little more paint.

As You Taste the Moon

I would like to understand how food
becomes a need, or a beautiful distraction,
like being seduced
by the fresh-baked, hot cornbread of desire
as I avoid life-changing decisions
when the glucose drops
below the level of self-respect

I make a funeral pyre
of all my well-intended dieting books,
take the ash
and cover the full temper of my body
before I swan dive
into the cold stream of reason,
or hang out at the graveyard
to celebrate with the spirits
on the day of the dead

This sacrament of food
feels like a transformational story,
a mindful inner digestion,
like a reflection on a deer print
in the willow break,
or the good, divine, and beautiful
when I behold you,
as you kiss and taste the moon
that swims upon the lake.

Mother Earth Speaks

I am at a quiet place, up canyon,
among the blue sky of oaks and
mexican jays,
the ancient whisper of stone
and the wingtip glide of falcon,
we feed one another,
give nourishment to the whole

The air tastes sweet here,
clean and confident
as the orbs of morning
pulse along the silk webs of spider woman,
each breath feels like becoming new

In the stillness I can hear her heart call

Last night over salad, she spoke
with her eyes,
"you know you belong here."

In the hush of moonlight I danced

*"Dear brother if you so choose
go to the big tree,
I will be there to help you
build a circle
we can pray together, sing, and heal."*

Grandfather's Boats

When summer rains filled the old wooden boats
my grandfather made,
I would rush to the river,
blade my way through the short cut,
all legs and arms tumbling down the steep hillside
to where the boats slumbered
half sunk at the river dock

These vessels and I, grateful for the bailing can,
how water felt heavy at the start,
lighter near the emptiness at the end,
as the river became more alive
with its fresh flow of remembering,
each mound of rusted chain
attached to a stone anchor,
to trust its hold to the river bottom
as my hands, like the stone,
spun whirlpools into the water's face

My body rowed these flat-bottom spirits
upon this waterway called Fox,
where I became free from a god
I lost faith in or believed
created lightning or thunder,
and yet I wondered about the fish
we harvested from the river,
was this god offering itself
into its own mystery of belonging?

These boats have all passed into the unknown
like my grandfather and all of his dreams,
I'm still rowing with the river
or at moments I drift and rest my oars into silence,
as a deer in moonlight calls out your name.

The First Dream

He reflected upon the first dream
there in the holy fluid of womb,
embryonic, without gravity
that flows through the great void,
with no fear or attachment
to become a somebody

Like liquid umber
moves along this river of stars,
like a galaxy pulses outward
yet into itself
beyond the abyss,
eternal and forever
unmeasured and unrehearsed
into a community of belonging

Is every dream the first dream
in the collective unconscious
that spirals like a ball of light
through the cleave of darkness?
the wild pulse and passion,
wet clay and sun's fire,
mass extinction and everlasting life

Shall we flow into the heart
that arises from compassion,
to emanate joy and delight?
an ideal that beholds
the beauty of every soul—
letting go of every dream,
of separation, to be right.

Less Attached

Today I felt hungry,
so after meditation
I went to the Dharma Supermarket,
food city to Nirvana

I did not know my own mind
so I filled the cart full of
religious objects like cat food,
prayer flags, donuts with and without
the hole, statues with Buddha on one side
and Guadalupe on the other,
and wisdom teachings
from Dr. Seuss and Charlie Brown

And then I renounced everything,
including renunciation,
and became a nobody,
holy ridiculous and suntanned

I drew a blue hole, like the sky,
around my belly button
so I would remember
that all is passing through me,
beyond clinging to desire and bliss,
or to wallow at the great wall of suffering

As I awaken from another dream
by the forest wild-water-stream,
to touch my heart in this riverbed
and feel less attached now
to the babble
inside my head.

In a Heron's Beak

A man watches a pair of crows
build a nest in the sky forest
from sticks and feathers
the fresh mud,
imprinted with deer tracks—
he waits in hunger
for what feels untamed and forgotten,
called out and mysterious

sun-life bleeds yellow and scarlet
into another day bed
of willow and moss,
ice crystals crackle, spill
into his blue flame of fire

as the other side of this world
sleeps into the spear-point of night,
to the call throat of mockingbird,
each wing beat of swan
that touches the moon

right beside
a set of mink tracks
a boy grew up wondering
how the river sand bottom
felt along his feet,
did one of these clams
contain a hidden pearl
to set him free?
or carry him away
like in a heron's beak.

"You learn to listen for comments that are the fingerprints of someone's personality."
— Karla Jennings

Silk or Ink

When i first read this line
"you learn to listen," bells from a
past religion trembled into my heart

when i first read this line
i wanted to steal it, paste it upon
the unseen wall of a previous life

when i first read this line
i thought the last word was *position,*
which made me feel too vulnerable about sex

when i first read this line
i wanted to smooch my own fingerprints and
not send them off to a once-forgotten lover

when i first read this line
i wanted to meet Karla in person, hand her
a silk thread and a comment about a rose

when i first read this line
for a moment someone else's personality
got in the way of how i prepare kale

when i first read this line
i realized there was no separation
between possibility and fingerpaint

when i first read this line
i knew nothing about sainthood
or what dries faster, silk or ink.

Gets Carved Out

She goes to the river,
sculpts the backbone of a poem
with the molars of her teeth
to soften the rawhide of memory,
the open vessel of truth

Her fingers press along clay
and the first green seed pods of maple,
a hummingbird lands on a heart
she painted upon her chest,
its beak touches her skin
drinks into the nectar of her soul

She smudges a stone
held warm in her hand
as it gives permission to drill
through its center,
to be shaped into a bead
or a bear, eagle, buffalo, snake

Her eyes flash toward a cricket
that leaps out of the marsh grass
lands in the water-pool
becomes a part of the trout
that leaves its splash and palette
upon the surface of surrender
like a smile from a forgotten friend

Like the raptor of a poem that rests
on the silver branch of a tree
as it gets carved out by
the chisel of wind and rain.

Be Silent Still

Ancient waters move underground
Recall that hum, that silent sound
What heals suffering, oh what may?
Some antidote like child's play

To gaze above the windowsill
A center point, a silent still
Where fear passes, gives up its thrill
From a softer voice a silent still

A bucket lifts from a dark-deep well
a distant sound, a ringing bell
From a place upon the hill
Be gentle now, oh silent still

Open this channel, connect the heart
As sky tears cleanse a forgotten part
Along the shore, each grain of sand
To join in circle pulse to hand

A mindful act to live in peace
At the center, to be released
And like a deer upon the hill
Oh grateful now, be silent still.

About to Fall

911 and a half is the street number
to the open bar of hope,
one light beer away from bliss
and just out of reach
from the stardust of judgment,
in the moral dilemma of hangovers

How the voices, the complaints
drift across the street,
the rehash of broken relationships,
lost in the cigarette glow
of one's own creation,
the liquid desire of connection,
a flash fantasy to find love

The ice age of a man watches,
like an unseen voyeur from across the way,
like a common tern stares at the sea

The neon sign flashes green, violet, pink,
orange, and blue, an invite to the waterhole,
how liquor softens the recall of
old shipwrecks,
the ground work of addiction,
the midday wish for a god
that cures the cancer of loneliness

The smoke heats and smolders
toward the shadow side of America,
same damn story, everyone wants to talk,
no one cares to listen or gaze skyward
to see that beautiful bomb
about to fall.

The Bones of It

I asked a Rinpoche
how he tempers his sexual desire,
he smiles and explains,
that in his lineage it is possible
to share in this form with another,
and then he clarifies
"it's easy not to act in this way,
when the need arises,
just look upon the person
as a skeleton."
I never thought of that,
as we both let out a belly laugh
spilling our tea

On my writer's desk is a postcard
of two skeletons,
as I glance at them
a soft grin chimes my face,
yet last night, as I unbolted the closet
of my mind in a dream,
the skeletons were taking pleasure
in all sorts of erotic positions,
in a play of ecstasy and grace
that began to make my own bones
quiver and shake,
as they gazed in my direction
shared a healthy chortle and said,
"do we ever let go
of our delight to celebrate?"

To Share

Can we practice our intuitive wisdom
as we commune with a raven
and a great horned owl
that lands in the olive tree,
moments apart
right above our gaze
into the morning engagement of blue?

We witness
as the sunrise water crystals
perch close to us,
like each way we feel in awe
by the blanket of flannel clouds
that fold about our body temple,
like silk spun around
the larva of our souls,
as raven and owl call out our names

There seems no distance now
between these two mountains
that can shield us
from winter's more silent pardon,
as a wish softens like grace
the violet flame of infinity,
you and I,
raven and owl,
such a beautiful day
to share a heart song.

Finish that Letter

As I write a letter
in the North Shore Café
on Lake Gitchegumee,
the cook appears like a daydream
between the white coffee mugs
and the unclean spoons
with a message on the back
of his tee shirt

NEVER FRY BACON NAKED

A slogan?
a tome of enlightenment
from an ancient text?
a catchphrase for the new age?

Was this a personal experience?
a kitchen ceremony
defrocked of pepper and salt?
does it hold true for all that gets folded
into the hot crackle of grease?
shall I test it out with the private spatula
of intimate friends?

Or go to the beach,
feed the oldest seagull
in the world instead,
continue to live,
and learn how to sail,
oh yeah!
finish that letter,
go slide it
in the mail.

The Moon

The moon dripped like a ripe mango
through the skylight of her dream
onto the wings of a lover,
as she felt the potential
of uncertainty, the vine of entanglement,
beauty beneath an underlayment of soul

Do all images become nectar
for the cosmic garden of desire,
to enjoy each flavor of the moon
that slips along the throat slide?

Does soul call forth the grace of humanity,
the dogma and duality of belief,
our rank of fear,
our need to heal into love?

At sunrise, she stares at a pile of stones
broken upon the hearth,
feels desperate to arrange them
into a pattern,
stack each one like a cairn
to mark the way, unknown

I know and I don't know blaze
along the timber frame of her mind,
past a sound that is half full, half empty
as a spark moves like a spiral
through the heart chamber of her belonging.

Planting Corn

I breathe to feel the tenderness
of your spirit-song
as you glean your hand into mine,
like an act of kindness, a sacrament
to the Beloved we meet everyday

What unfolds within the bounty
of each season
as warm rain and sunlight
press along the grotto of your heart?

As you plant the first kernels
of blue corn
where your fingers mingle deeper
into mine,
as your innocent child-self
reclaims the sparkle of this earth
that rejoices from the songs
in your hands.

Peg Leg

In the blade of morning
at the outdoor food bank
I start to bemoan the cold,
dressed for the sun that had yet to arrive,
to put on a few attempts at gratitude
keep my discomfort
under shelter, the other side,
as I observe the mind
and its desire to complain
about my chilled body
to every passerby.

A woman limps up beside me,
"could you fill out this form for me, please?"
yes indeed I reply,
as she pulls up her pant leg and smiles,
"Peg Leg Meg is my name,"
knocking on her artificial thigh,
I grin back
and give in, to a deeper sigh.

Belonging

I belong to you tree,
smooth limbed in childhood,
as I climb into your arms,
high view and protected

I belong to you sap,
dried and amber
or fresh and transparent
bonds to my fingerprints

I belong to you tree,
your bark-skin scent
pressing into mine
grooved and heartwood

I belong to you leaves,
that shade my body
crow nest and bird song
pollen paint and pine-nut

I belong to you tree,
when I hug you there
deep forest and evergreen
skyward and sacred

I belong to you roots,
buried and hungered
feeling into darkness
humus and clay-bank

I belong to you, tree, in life and death
forever grateful to the soil and the seed,
thunder stick and rain cloud
moon branch and buffalo hide
sundog— circle wide.

I Get Desperate

I only get desperate now
when the cat-claw thorn
breaks off into my finger skin
blood prick and ice thin

I get desperate
when the messenger arrives
and I say, "I'm not ready now"
bouncing off the light beam
half naked and orange peeled

I get desperate
clinging to the bow spirit
through fractured soul of love
cracking into north wind
old bones below and new bones above

I get desperate
in the cave dream of thought
feeling like a lightning bolt
that bullet in the dark
hawk cry and willow break

I get desperate
when I see your eyes
melt into mine like an animal skin,
dopamine and water-pool
fire-flame and earthquake
sunspots and moon lake
tongue whisper and belly snake.

The Big Empty

I strive to fill the dark,
the Big, Dark, Empty

to seal it with love I claim
the grief of tears I choose to name
the smoke, the timber, the fire flame
in the Big, Dark, Empty

to seek its source and fill it up
like Noah's ark or a silver cup
a wild pitch, a change-up
to the Big, Dark, Empty

to pack this life with you and me
in my passion to conceive,
but I never felt complete to be
in the Big, Dark, Empty

to fill it from the waterfall park
one splash closer to the center mark
to taste so sweet, a bitter spark
of the Big, Dark, Empty

with nothing less than all of that
spinning clouds like acrobats
with all my life a habitat
the poisoned arrow, the miner's shaft
round and round I command this craft

through the Big, Dark, Empty,
through the Big, Dark, Empty.

The Golden Laughter

It feels like the ease
in which we smell
the lemon's glow,
the unfiltered words
lifted over the table
between the curried teeth
of crunchy cheese curds
and the open trumpets
of daffodils

How the soft swill
of spring water,
the moderate pearl
of red wine
relaxes the amygdala,
as joy can enter
the golden laughter
of our souls.

Giving Birth

I pocket lines
from the great poets,
like rabbit, hawk,
squeaky mouse, and timber-doodle,
shape the fur and feathers
into my own symbols of the unknown
like a medicine wheel of wings
attached to stars

I borrow from the noble voices
of grizzly bear, buffalo, elk, and raven
into a web of dreams
the heartbeat of muscle and bone
like a song can hibernate into the soul

I receive messages
from mink, muskrat, fox, and badger
their tracks lead into the shelters
of our ancestors,
to the imprints of petroglyphs,
to moon and sun

Yet still I wonder how much is true
what words to shape toward the new,
as in the warm moon of night
to watch a deer lay curled from sight
giving life, new birth,
this divine moment,
Oh Beloved! Sacred Earth.

Beauty

Was it more than just Nabokov who
suffered from his knowledge
that he could not "swallow
all the beauty in this world"
or assimilate all such splendor
through the open blades of his novels,
the pollen prints of his poetry to Vera?

Steal lines from the great writers,
I was told, and make them your own,
thus I began to pleat them out
like cabbages give way to sauerkraut,
poured the entangled verb of love,
inside of beauty,
into a glass of cabernet,
looked beyond beauty as a noun
from a summer parade

yet beauty in its charm,
its palomino skin,
the lace wing of its heart,
slipped out from my open hand
like a metaphor can pass unseen
through the dark

not because I had my eyes closed
or my mind draped full of desire
to simply behold you, oh beauty thee

that by letting go
you will return
eternal, beauty be.

Share Your Best

A poet laureate at the workshop said,
"don't write about love,"
so I wrote about garbage cans,
how sunlight creates shadow,
bridges I crossed over
that jumped me into rivers,
and the devil's flaming underwear

I wrote about social change
quarters, dimes, and nickels
the endless ways we lose the thread
what we all believe about the pickle

how we get trapped into a cage
hideaway our entangled rage,
like a rigid vow forevermore
do we steel gate and bolt the door?

Yet heart keeps sounding
inside the chest,
wake up my darling
share your best,
go write about love
and the soul's sweet glimmer,
shine your life
like starlight, shimmer.

The Un-shamed

Today
sunlight flowed
into her heart
as she embraced
and gifted
the un-shamed
glow of herself
into her divine essence,
like a smile
shared in silence,
like a kind voice
within a whisper,
like a silk thread
spun inside the soul.

As Love Awakes

Where Earth quakes
the dawn star breaks
each day spark flakes
a wave a wake
what spirit bakes
inside of you
inside of you

every emotion slakes
as the heart thirst takes
each kiss it makes
where your fingers rake
for divine sake
inside of you
inside of you

no one can fake
how hips will shake
where water snakes
into source of lake
as love awakes
inside of you
inside of you.

The Foxes

I watched the two red foxes
out in meadow hay
they looked in my direction
smiled and said, come play

I was only five years old then
when I first heard their voice
I quickly ran and joined them
it felt like the perfect choice

We ran across the prairie
and jumped the little creeks
we soon became best friends
in this game of hide and seek

They taught me about silence
and a gentle way to listen
to the voice of grandma singing
baking muffins in her kitchen

They displayed acts of kindness
that nature is a friend
and to share gifts together
creates a joyful trend

They spoke of being open
to the spirit in all things
that magic is creation
to trust your voice to sing

So I sang to the foxes
to the community of life
Oh! thank you wild foxes
for your playful sweet advice.

Sing to the Stones

When he goes out on a pilgrimage
not to Rome, Machu Picchu,
or the pyramids at Giza,
with no need to dress in white or black
to seek out salvation, suffering,
or resurrection

He walks alone instead
with sky as his witness,
clothed or not in a way unknown,
to the fine stone edge
of Pumpkin Seed Point,
flint-napped by sun and wind
and the talon scrapings
of golden eagles

He draws a circle
with a stone or stick,
lies still inside
until the first sun arrives,
until the moon
falls into his eyes

Afterwards
he ate squash
and popcorn soup,
sang songs to the stones
in the rain.

Brain Fog

It's unpleasant
to wake up in a brain fog,
food can help, if one remembers how to eat

These moments in the fog I hole up
in the arms of shelter
with hot tea, a bed, the swirl of tears
waiting for the pain body to pass

To go out into the world in such a haze
invites disaster,
like a ship navigating in a storm
without anyone at the helm

Yet so little seems to happen in this void,
this thick curl of smoke
where all worlds get sucked up,
dreams become incomplete,
I no longer remember
how doors open or close,
what it is I keep staring at,
how to get from here to there
to recall the names of friends
or anything that appears solid

In time it burns away
as I feel the essence of who I am
to belong in the world,
grateful for what gets left behind,
and to laugh, listen, and love again.

"I'm one of those people that can live with one way of doing things only for a short time. I'm very experimental." Allan Houser

Take the Wax Away

Once everything seemed created from smoke,
the first bones and the tissue that
brought them together.
This was all experimental,
—long before ink,
close to a transition period of
charcoal and stone.
Like symbols in clouds,
the whirlpools of rivers,
and when stars spoke out
all the original names.
Like a dream
moving on its own water.
Experiential
like silver inlayed into fire,
as intuition shapes the clay,
how the thirst of a woman
gave birth to light and thunder,
speaks in the tongues of red willow,
allows the sweet heat to take the wax away.

Elemental Gifts

Water is like the embryonic fluid of life
how we tender our lips in a cold spring
the way each moon floats upon the lake
as we swim into the ink of darkness
that mirrors the tremble of the awakened soul

Air is like wing tips in the voices of wind,
carves out sandstone arches and alcoves,
deepens into the fabric of our lungs
to breathe in and out
a mystery of soul

Earth is like the grounding
a temporal touch into the land of soul
as clay gets shaped like our bodies
how decay makes humus
where the green moss grows

Fire is like a blue blaze of transformation
burns away what no longer serves,
fire can germinate the dormant seed,
sparks and warms the soul
into a place of belonging

Fire flame is older than memory,
sacred earth is home to everything changing,
clean water sustains a healthy life force,
pure air is breath shared
renews itself with all of creation—
let us respect these elemental gifts
and nurture the divine essence
of every living soul.

A Place

There is a place on earth called Iowa
where everything turns green
and wet puddles sparkle like geese
circling the moon

    a place that comforts blue corn,
the once-forgotten memories
of heirloom squash,
where voices of deer and eagle,
crane and frog
still speak in their indigenous tongues

a place to enter the water dipper
of truth and understanding
as you cross that bridge
over the Big River

everyone back home believes
they know all about
your return to such a place
close to where you were born,
like the height of your shadow
the illumined presence of your light,
as you arrive like a sound from creation,
to awaken from the soul's
dark night.

Gratitude

*I just want to thank you,
gratitude fills my heart*

These are half of the words
from a chant I am singing today
as I walk, drive, sit

It feels good to sing
like placing my feet in warm water
to touch upon
what gentleness, kindness,
gratitude, and forgiveness can bring

*With all the goodness and
abundance you bestow*

This is the rest of the chant,
I don't know who wrote it

It's enough, in this moment,
in this day to sing
as I call forth your divine name.

The Big Heat

When I walk into the wild places
where the saguaros bloom
I start to enter The Big Heat,
I step along the weave of a dry wash
share footfalls with tortoise,
rattlesnake, and gila monster,
my cousins on four legs, coyote and mountain lion,
I leave all fear at the quick stop,
welcome the wisdom of
black widow spider, scorpion, and tarantula,
I ponder my existence, my dry laughter,
the limber of old age
and to forgive myself and anyone
that I believed betrayed me,
as I find fresh solitude in The Big Heat

Past midday the sun burns high
in the wings of its worship,
there are no other human tracks off trail
where the frame of me snuggles into the shade
of a favorite tree,
my hand discovers a stone in the shape of a heart
as I reach for the one inside my chest
kissing it with my fingertips,
small gnats press into every orifice
of my body that is unprotected,
I wonder, how faraway the wind is,
I make a small circle out of stones and deer bones,
horse hair and cornmeal,
pray onto the fabric of my skin in soft sand
to Earth Mother and Sky Father,
my heart and spirit evolve in these wild places
all else can become, a beautiful distraction.

Sing Underwater

What's it like
to practice and play
in the field of kindness?
tape butterfly wings
we have found
to the nimble breath
of our fingertips

What's it like to walk backwards?
review our angled attachments
to the past,
or write love letters to ourselves
and mail them from various places
we wish to inhabit

Can we un-pretend we are someone
other than ourselves?
change our name
using letters from an alphabet
that has yet to be invented

Sing underwater,
ditch the fork in the road,
start at the end
and end at the beginning,
leave early and arrive late,
then dance, dance, dance,
spin, spin, spin,
remove the hard pits from the center
before we share the sweetest dates.

Forgiveness

I live in the world
no need to pretend
I know something
or have an answer
for the continuation of
another living soul

Today I feel the greasewood
pray in its native tongue
like the way sycamore leaves
hum to the holy blue-void,
like water and fire
that join together in a dream

If there is a path
to heal into wholeness
it might enter
from the breath of forgiveness,
like an echo from the sun
to the heart,
how the nerves respond to everything,
like darkness and light

As we move on
like fire burns the land,
we lay down upon the earth,
embrace the center of our hearts,
and nurture the sanctity of soul,
loving all the parts.

On Her Body

Have you seen the booklet of haikus
she wrote back in the sixties?
when she believed Li Po and Basho knew
something about three lines and no waiting

She wrote them with broken crayons
each word a new color,
some were written backwards or layered
like a chocolate cake

She pinned them to the wheels of my bicycle
so they would spin like prayers
through the small midwest town
of rivers and churches, taverns and sand-hills

She read them to chipmunks,
and to bluegills that spawned under the bridge,
left them in the nests of mourning doves
and half folded in the money basket at church

She wrote them like spirals
of campfire smoke, dipped them into paint
and the open lips of clams

In season she used mulberries and
mink tracks in place of words,
raindrops on her tongue and
bones from owl pellets

She did not sell them for ten cents each
like packages of radish seeds,
but laid them on her body
like a green cloverleaf.

My Silver Key

Poems become marker points to my heart
a guide to my ancestors
stone carvers and Goddess worshipers

Poems are my seedbed, clay and loam,
sandstone and pictograph
memory turned over
cultivated with turtle and snake, raven and
otter

Poems are the birthstones of my afterlife
free falling like a leaf
at the first harvest moon of Autumn

Poems wake up inside of me
like a water spring from a mountain
bubbles out from my thirsty soul

Poems are my shield
along the nerve bone of rage,
the cold, blind steel of fear
the bite of the underdog

Poems are my burial ground
and silent resurrection,
the present moment I give value to,
in a vision to fly free

Poems are my wings
my silver key
my warm sparkle of thread
out of the darkness.

Light Changes Everything

The mountain shadow speaks
through the contours of tree limbs
and gray-white clouds
that shape themselves into animal totems
like the leap of faith of antelope or deer
like the shell back of turtle island

spirits at dawn feel gentle now
echo their voices into a softness
like a small patch of frost
on the tender green

silhouettes of birds rush by,
skip, like well-shaped stones,
along the first reach of sky,
then disappear
into the pool like mountain earth

light changes everything
like a message from your own prayer
tethered to a kite or a cloud,
like an image as we emerge
from the water spring,
that steam of earth—
fresh, unplowed.

The Wind

The wind feels like a desire
crossing over
from one mind into another,
as the dust devils coil
across dry lake beds
and carry thoughts
like seed pollen
into the thick city night,
where crows roost on a
brick building of light and thunder,
or on the lake edge
where a Wilderness can sleep into us
alone and unafraid

crow and wind
their forms seem to swallow all secrets,
how they layer the sky
blue-black like infinity,
their beaks talk in silver-gold
near a place we walk
between prayer and pleasure,
the unknown and unknowable

the crow-wind stops our throats
from speaking,
we listen at the near hum of silence,
a fledgling tips forward from the nest,
suspended for a moment, like all of us,
to share our very best.

To Be Holy

When you call on your best friend
or your higher self,
is that a toll-free number?

when you speak about a marker point
in your life path,
is it positive, negative, or gender neutral?

when you wake up in the morning,
is the first breath you become aware of
moving in or out?

how many angels sleep with you
through any given night?

have you ever felt neutrinos
moving through your bath water?

how often do you sing or dance
unattached to whoever is watching?

do you communicate with aliens
during spiritual or religious practices?

do you remember how to fly or shape shift,
at least in your dreams?

did you ever ride a bicycle
without using your hands?
or smooch your fingers
into the lay of wet sand?
to be holy with all
that we may never, ever understand.

Shall We Share?

Do we all make up reasons
to be alone?
then gather up to share cornbread
get intimate with our favorite friends

does the sun's fire
bake through the window of memory
where emotions can be difficult to unwrap,
like duct tape that sticks to itself
or love that we shy away from

like a mountain lion we never see
can outline our lives
like the blue sky
we long to become a part of

at night
does the day drip away from everything
that spools out of our mouth,
wets the pillow before we awaken
from the image, when raven and snake
become one in our memory

what is
may never be explained,
and what is not might move
in the opposite direction of tomorrow

shall we share
the abundance from our life?
will we articulate
the boundless gratitude of our belonging?

Drink Good Water

What heals into our bones,
cleanses the wounds of our ancestors?
speaks to our hearts
like the flow of life
inward and outward?
like a circle,
a spiral,
a drink of good water
into the purity and thirst
of our soul.

What is Love?

She fancied her desire
to write about love,
like an ocean wave pleats
the inner shoreline of the heart,
the forever-beloved kiss,
of earth and sun

what is not love?
a list of promises that got broken,
lockdown of the heart,
our confused thoughts
like judgment and hate,
our vengeance
when we become unforgiving

is it all love?
our separation and our union
our internal war and peace
to give and withhold
our distance and our closeness

does love pass like a flame
that burns away the wood?
eternal and beholding
unknown and unspeakable
that moment of surrender
a practice of kindness
in any given moment
for the highest good.

To Aim Skyward

He paid cash for a fig tree last night
two days before
the full blood moon of Autumn,
and received downloads of guidance
on how to plant and care for
this two-year-old called "Brown Turkey"
that he soon forgot
as dawn spilled along Sacred Mountain

He heard it gobble as he first laid eyes
upon its six leaves,
which seem incapable
of covering what is private,
like thoughts
or certain flashes of skin tone

He sat outside beside her
to caress the moment of her leaves
unexpected like burlap,
his fingers feel her stretch of bark
as his heart beholds her dormant bud
that aims skyward
like a myth, a new vision of heaven,
ready to be planted
here on earth.

The Mind Palace

Early, before the sun
splashes light into the mind's eye,
I mow around the kitchen barefoot,
spill water on the counter,
down into my robe sleeve
and along the floor,
a timeless moment
like it would never stop
into forever

A tangerine lies on the top of an apple,
for a head, a cherry would be fine,
now I have a human companion
to share the dark-roasted coffee morning

I am visiting the cactus, mesquite,
and succulents of the city
as I wonder about the holy trinity—
how did I get here, where am I going,
and who am I now?

I could escape into the mind palace
of Sherlock Holmes, but even that seems
limited or a bit boring after a vigorous
sunbath in the desert heat and, besides,
who needs more drama and addiction?

The spilled water calls for attention
as I finish cleansing
the under souls of my feet.

At The Canyon

If I painted the Canyon with words
i would start with burnt charcoal
of Ponderosa Pine and the vein sap of Doug Fir

it would be from lichens that speak in moonlight,
flint chips of white and red bedrock,
echoes from our blood memory

it would score and scour like the underbelly
of the falcon's cry
talons that can open a wounded heart

it would be in the tongue call of elk
to mate in a harvest season
of pinenut and firewood

it would be in the cold snake of river
cottonwood and sandbar,
a drink from raven's beak

it would be how the sun storms into a rock shelter
turquoise and pictographs
finger-marks in clay our ancestors shaped

it would be in the call of canyon wren
and all that must go unnamed

it would be in everything
I could rub on my skin from this Earth,
gather and shape in gratitude
with the blades of my hands
and the wind-breath of my soul.

Inclusive and Free

Underneath the alcoves
are deep like sounds of the primordial ones—
grinding stones and corn
the kivas of Anasazi dreams

Capitol Gorge, San Rafael Swell, and Grand Gulch,
names placed on a map like thumbprints
in the Wilderness, in the glazed patina of
sandstone

The ancestral language of original poetry
lies covered and infused in bedrock
as it waits for the complete recovery
of wolf, condor, mountain lion, and grizzly bear,
whooping crane and leopard frog—
for their full return
inclusive and free into the tapestry of the land,
maybe they will be kinder to us
than we have been to them
and teach us how to leap, fly, sing, and play again

The sediments wish to speak,
but it takes days lying on the earth skin,
underneath a cottonwood by the water seep
bare of chest and full of thirst to listen

It's no mistake when you palm your hands
onto the prints of the ancient ones
or how deep you submerge your own limbs
into the memory of a clay bank,
soft and wet with rain,
how your prints rest there until the archaic poems
bleed up into your fingers, along your tender arms,
into the *rincon* of your sacred heart.

Paradox Tabernacle

Your dream is everyone's dream
pleated along the chalice of duality,
what transcends into the world
between darkness and light?

The mystic travels
through a barnyard of beliefs,
while the mind babble goes on
like a thunder cloud trembles
at its own form, through the dry arroyo

Can we think our way out of this myth,
removed from the house we were raised in?
that dream in the parents' bedroom
their secrets and unrehearsed sounds of rain,
who bellies up to original sin anymore?

We separated like cream from milk
clinging to some knowledge, some belief
we use as shields, to hide our doubts,
our spiritual images into belonging

We climb the steps to a soothsayer
to interpret the wound of our psyche,
the meaning behind the dream,
as a coyote muscles around the corner
with a feral cat in its teeth

We shudder, unspoken, in that moment
as the "paradox tabernacle" opens
as we give back the host from our beaks.

What to Consider

I no longer consider myself a religious person
though I've heard Eternity
singing through the branches of trees
with names like spruce,
chestnut, eucalyptus and bristlecone pine—
in the enchanted voice of a canyon wren,
song sparrow, meadowlark, and loon call

I do not consider myself to be an idol worshiper
yet I feel the Divine
in the angelic buzz of cricket and cicada,
tree frog, and sounds without names

I listen to Spirit speak
in the still mountain silence of Wilderness,
in the deepest, water-pocket fold of the soul

I witness God cry
in the dark pain of grief and suffering,
held in the terror of my own arms
from the fear and shadow of remembering

I paddle in the canoe of your love charm
as I pray with the family of all creation
and wrap a piece of your stone and feather
into the twist of my hair

I savor you, Beloved,
in the unpolluted water spring
in the flame that makes the jack pine grow

I see you, Dear One,
in every form of life and death
as I behold you, in a moment,
timeless within the breath.

Another Life

He walks through the market
in a fantasy of pleasure,
he forgets to pick up
a pound of carrots,
or a pound of flesh

some other possibility
in the scent of cloves, wool,
garlic, chilies, and camel dung

like a tin of fine smokes
for a tobacco give away,
as the heart of him leaps
toward the color of your whisper,
into a sunrise song unbounded,
where Mercury spins out of retrograde
and Venus rises, untethered.

Shift and Stretch

When you become still
what calls forth
from the memory of your eyes?
what sighs
from the window of your breath?

In a trance
you wrapped your body in thin gauze
where he could no longer see you,
or discern such layers of muscle and bone,
each weave made the past disappear
like wind moves sand into water

This transparency of a human life,
uplifts and unfolds
as two tectonic plates
shift and stretch to the light.

Playful with the Earth

Here I am, looking out a window
lusting after a breast,
as if my one-year-old could suckle
into its need of comfort and belonging

here I am, a teen on the threshold
of suicide, depression, and sex
as if a lightning bolt from this storm
could strike open my soul

here I am, in my twenties
waking up from a night of abuse,
as if a hangover could stumble me
toward a healing

here I am, in my thirties
to upgrade my addictions,
build a medicine wheel,
lie down in the center to awaken my heart

here I am, divorced in my forties
the walking wounded
the dark night of soul
the native tears of ruptured bliss

here I am, at fifty-five
loved and healed, blessed and whole
filtering out the chaff of my poetry
with bird songs and otter tracks

here I arrive, in my sixties
laughing with the universe
flowing with the river
playful on the earth
dancing in the sky.

The Stones Speak

She heard from the stones
that in another time
more ancient than atoms,
when love went away
to hide, lost its memory,
its songs and rituals—
that the earth wept
and stopped spinning
in its grief to share with love
its divine essence,
whole and self-realized.

As We Behold

My favorite dreams
are made from buffalo hump and seal fat
beaver tail and wild berries

My favorite dreams
recall the old dances, movement of my feet,
the thunderbird and the lightning stick,
bone whistle and eagle wing

My favorite dreams
are from the drippings of maple tree sap,
spring water from the side ache
of no-name mountain

My favorite dreams
evoke the virtues of our ancestors,
their flint tools and ring of fire,
goddess worship and stone carver

My favorite dreams
are from the smells I cannot see
the sounds, not of teeth,
long before the bow and arrow

My favorite dreams
invite a healing from the drumbeat
within the field chambers of every heart,
as we beckon and behold the starlight
of every living soul.

Untitled

the gentle wing-makers
good spirits with opened eyes
feel love upon their skin

Where I Go To Lie Down

Please do not tell anyone
how slow I travel along
the woods and deserts of forever,
off trail, away from the stampede
where the crowd goes crazy,
forgets what is wild

Please do not attempt to explain me when I
place my fingers into the cleave of deer tracks,
pick apart the marbled dreams of owl pellets,
press my nose beside the ribs of earth
take in the vapors of clay, sand and loam,
wrap my temple around ponderosa pines
breathe in their scent of vanilla,
how I cleave my hands around their torsos,
kiss them all, as if they are living saints

Please refrain from telling anyone
what unfolds between me
and the muscles of river clams,
where I must go alone to find blue sky
and nurture the seed skin of my soul,
like a place to swim
within and beyond this wild earth
to enter the open field of the soul

Please do not even whisper
where I go to lie down in a buffalo wallow,
to sing my heart song and to pray.

Made in the USA
Columbia, SC
15 January 2018